A Brief Introduction to Islam

Jamaal Diwan

To my wife, my teacher, for her wisdom, patience, and unwavering support.

To my parents, my dear sister, and Greg for their love.

To Ismail.

About the Author

Jamaal Diwan received a Bachelor's Degree in Third World Studies from the University of California, San Diego in 2005. He then traveled to Egypt where he spent the next 6 years studying Arabic and Islamic Studies. In 2012 he completed a law degree in Sharia from al-Azhar University in Cairo. While in Egypt he also began an MA program in Islamic Studies at the American University in Cairo but was not able to complete it due to the revolution in 2011. He is a regular speaker at local universities on issues pertaining to Islam and Muslims in America and some of his writings have been published in the OC Register and other newspapers. He can be followed on Twitter @jamaaldiwan

Contents

Introduction

There is no shortage of misinformation around the beliefs of Islam and Muslims. Some misinformation is intentional and some unintentional, some propagated by Muslims themselves and some by those who do not subscribe to the teachings of Islam. This short text is meant to be a brief, yet thorough introduction to what Muslims actually believe.

To the general audience, I hope that you will find this text simple, straightforward, and not overwhelming. The breadth and depth of Muslim scholarship throughout history is vast and I've done my best here to try and stick to the most important and foundational questions and particularly the things that I have found to repeat themselves in my years of studying and teaching Islam. In the first draft I found myself repeating often "Muslims believe…" It is tedious to read that over and over again so I took it out. My hope is that you will read the entire text with the phrase "Muslims believe" in front of it. The nuance here is to explain what we believe in firmly and with absolute conviction while at the same time not giving the impression that we are trying to force those beliefs on others.

To the Muslim audience, I hope that this text will serve as a quick refresher and reminder of the most basic teachings of our faith. I also hope that those new Muslims who come across this text will find it simple and easy to understand. This is the core of our faith, we must not forget it. I have done my best to use the most reliable of information although I have not cited my sources in detail. I did not want to make the text overly academic. Any Prophetic tradition that is included in here is considered to be reliable by scholars of hadith unless otherwise noted. I have also refrained from the customary "peace be upon him" that is to be stated after mentioning any of God's prophets. This is not out of disrespect or negligence but simply to facilitate the read. It is expected that Muslims will make the appropriate supplication when passing over the names of the Prophets, may God's peace and blessings be upon all of them.

What is Islam?

The word *islam* is an Arabic word and most Arabic words revolve around consonant-based roots. In this case the root letters are *s-l-m*. The constellation of words that revolves around this root shares certain meanings. The most common of them are peace, tranquility, submission, and surrender. It is for this reason that Muslims generally perceive Islam to be a way of peace and submission, or, more particularly, they look at Islam as the way by which one achieves peace by submitting to God. The word *Islam* refers to the religion itself while the word *Muslim* refers to the person who practices the religion. As such, we would say that a person is Muslim but not that they are Islam or Islamic.

Islam, as practiced by over a billion people all around the world, refers to much more than this simple definition. It is the way of submitting to God that is known through the teachings of God Himself in the Quran.[1] These teachings are exemplified by the lived example of Muhammad. Muslims believe that these two sources of

---

[1] The Quran is the holy book of Islam. It will be covered in much detail in the section on the scriptures that were sent to different prophets.

inspiration provide the necessary guidance for human beings in all areas of their lives, whether directly or indirectly. All of the areas of Islamic Studies that impact the practical guidance of Islam in people's daily lives are derived from these sources and the entire body of Muslim scholarship is an ongoing attempt to faithfully interpret these texts.

What Do Muslims Believe?

There are six major beliefs that every Muslim must believe in if they are to be considered a Muslim. These six beliefs are the foundations of faith. Let us go through them one at a time.

I. God is One

The most important belief in Islam is the oneness of God. God has no sons, partners, intermediaries, or similitude. He is simply God, the Infinite, the Absolute. He is the same God as the God of Christianity and Judaism and any other monotheistic belief system. God, Who created the heavens and the earth and all that exists therein.

God has infinite names, some of which have been revealed to mankind through messengers and inspiration. God is the Just, the Merciful, the Powerful, the Knowledgeable, the Loving, the Forgiving, and so on.

There are many parts of the Quran which are clear on this issue and give descriptions of God as the Creator and Sustainer of all things. For example, God says about Himself in the Quran[2]:

> "Whatever is in the heavens and the earth exalts God, and He is the Exalted in Might, the Wise. His is the dominion of the heavens and the earth. He gives life and causes death and He is over all things competent. He is the First and the Last, the Ascendant and the Intimate, and He is, of all things, Knowing. It is He who created the heavens and earth in six days and then established Himself on the Throne. He knows what penetrates into the earth and what emerges from it and what descends from heaven and what ascends therein; and He is with you wherever you are. And God, of what you do, is Seeing. His is the dominion of the heaven and the earth. And to God are returned all matters. He causes

---

[2] For Muslims the Quran is the direct word of God. Sometimes I will say "the Quran says about this" and sometimes I will say "God says in the Quran." Either way it should be understood to mean that this is, for the Muslim, the direct statement of God. It is only being expressed in different ways.

the night to enter the day and the day to enter the night, and He is the Knowing of that within the hearts."[3]

He also says in another place:

"He is God, other than whom there is no deity, Knower of the unseen and the witnessed. He is the Entirely Merciful, the Especially Merciful. He is God, other than whom there is no deity, the Sovereign, the Pure, the Perfect, the Bestower of Faith, the Overseer, the Exalted in Might, the Compeller, the Superior. Exalted is God above whatever they associate with Him. He is God, the Creator, the Inventor, the Fashioner; to Him belong the best names. Whatever is in the heavens and earth is exalting Him. And He is the Exalted in Might, the Wise."[4]

Some of the other names of God are: the Source of Peace, the Creator, the Sustainer, the Giver of All, the Inspirer of

---

[3] Quran 57:1-6.
[4] Quran 59: 22-24.

Faith, the Magnificent, the Mighty, the Generous, the Truth, the Possessor of All Strength, the Originator, the Glorious, and many more.

The principle of the oneness of God is the most foundational principle of the teachings of Islam and Islam is a strictly monotheistic message. As the Quran says, "There is nothing like unto Him, and He is the Hearing, the Seeing."[5]

II. God Created Angels and They Exist

The second major belief in Islam is in the existence of angels. Angels are a creation of God separate from human beings, they are created from light, and they do as He commands them without any sort of disobedience. The Quran says about this, "They do not disobey God in what He commands them and they do as He commands."[6]

One of the results of believing that angels are a separate creation from human beings is to not believe that

---

[5] Quran 42:11.
[6] Quran 66:6.

human beings die and become angels. Angels and human beings are two separate beings and neither becomes the other. If human beings go to heaven, they go as human beings and not angels.

Angels do not disobey God but rather do whatever He tells them to do. Therefore, Satan is not a fallen angel. Rather, Satan belongs to a different group of creation called the Jin. The Jin are a third type of creation of God who have independent thought and free will. They are created from smokeless fire and can see human beings but humans cannot see them. The Quran says about this, "Indeed, he [Satan] sees you, he and his tribe, from where you do not see them."[7]

Together the angels and the Jin make up a large portion of the "unseen;" that which we believe exists because of what we are told in revelation but we do not see with our naked eye.

---

[7] Quran 7:27.

III. God Sent Messengers to Mankind

The next major belief in Islam is that God sent
messengers to mankind throughout history. Islam affirms
many of the same prophets and messengers as the Judeo-
Christian tradition such as Adam, Noah, Abraham, Isaac,
Jacob, Joseph, David, Solomon, and Moses. Muslims also
believe in Jesus, but not as the son of God. Islam teaches
that he was a messenger similar to the ones that came
before him and one of the greatest of the messengers
without a doubt. God makes special mention in the Quran
of a group of messengers that are considered to be the
greatest of the messengers. Jesus is included in this group.
He says, "And [mention, O Muhammad], when We took
from the prophets their covenant and from you and from
Noah and Abraham and Moses and Jesus, the son of Mary;
and We took from them a solemn covenant."[8] The human
nature of Jesus is also why the one who reads the Quran
will find him mentioned over and over again as "the son of
Mary," in order to clarify the Muslim belief that Jesus is a
great prophet but not the son of God. All the prophets were
sent with the same general message of worshipping one
God and doing good deeds and the total number of prophets

---

[8] Quran 33:7.

sent to mankind far exceeds the number of those mentioned in the Quran and the prophetic traditions, perhaps even reaching over 120,000. The Quran says about this:

> "Indeed, We have revealed to you [Muhammad], as We revealed to Noah and the prophets after him. And We revealed to Abraham, Ishmael, Isaac, Jacob, the Descendents, Jesus, Job, Aaron, and Solomon, and to David We gave the book [the Psalms]. And [We sent] messengers about whom We have related [their stories] to you before and messengers about whom We have not related to you. And God spoke to Moses with [direct] speech. [We sent] messengers as bringers of glad tidings and warners so that mankind will have no argument against God after the messengers. And ever is God Exalted in Might and Wise."[9]

These messengers were sent to all kinds of different people in various places and times. God says about this in the

---

[9] Quran 4:163-165.

Quran, "And there was no nation but that there had passed within it a warner."[10]

Prophets were the best of examples for mankind and therefore did not commit sins. They were protected by God in their missions and did not engage in ignoble behavior. This is a point of major difference between how Muslims understand the prophets and how some of the prophets of God are spoken about in what are today known as the Old and New Testaments. Let us take the story of David and Bathsheba which is mentioned in the Old Testament as an example.[11] In the Old Testament it says that David looked out upon the city and saw a beautiful woman bathing. After seeing her he called upon her and slept with her, after which she became pregnant. He tried to get her husband to sleep with her but he refused to do so because he was a soldier and the rest of his companions were at battle. After this failed attempt it is said that David instructed for him to be sent to the front lines where he would be killed in battle and after that he married the woman. In the Muslim belief system this is a completely unacceptable story because a Prophet of God is the ultimate

---

[10] Quran 35:24.
[11] See 2 Samuel 11.

human example of every noble and good quality that can be manifested in the human race, and it ties into the question of preservation of scripture and the finality of the Quran as the only reliable scripture for mankind, which will be discussed in the next section.

Messengers and prophets were sent with miracles, given to them by God, to prove their prophethood. These miracles were not from their own doing and were in contradiction to the normal rules of life. We believe that these miracles were specific and related to the time that the prophets lived in, except in the case of Muhammad. For example, in the time of Moses people were very interested in magic and sorcery. For this reason when God sent Moses to Pharaoh he sent him with a few miracles that were similar in appearance to magic; namely, he turned his staff into a serpent and his hand would become glowing white when removed from his pocket. To the common person these seemed like magic tricks and so when Pharaoh saw these miracles he summoned all of the greatest sorcerers he could find to have a showdown with Moses. The sorcerers could recognize the difference between their tricks and the true miracle that Moses was blessed to perform and accepted his message immediately. The Quran tells this story in detail:

> "And when the magicians arrived they said to Pharaoh, 'Is there indeed a reward for us if we are victorious?' He said, 'Yes, and indeed, you will then be of those who are near to me.' Moses said to them, 'Throw whatever you will throw.' So they threw their ropes and their staffs and said, 'By the might of Pharaoh, indeed it is we who will be victorious.' Then Moses threw his staff and at once it devoured what they falsified. So the magicians fell down in prostration to God. They said, 'We have believed in the Lord of the worlds, the Lord of Moses and Aaron.'"[12]

So in this case Moses was sent with a miracle that was related to what was on the minds of the people of his time so it was an easy means of convincing them as to the truth of his prophethood. The same can be said about Jesus.

---

[12] Quran 26:41-48.

In the time of Jesus people were very interested in issues related to healing and medicine. As such the miracles that he was given related to those interests. Specifically, he was able to cure the ill, heal the blind, cure the leper, and bring the dead back to life, all by the will of God. Jesus is actually reported by God in the Quran to have said this himself:

> "And a messenger to the Children of Israel, [who will say], 'Indeed I have come to you with a sign from your Lord in that I design for you from clay like the form of a bird, then I breathe into it and it becomes a bird by the permission of God. And I cure the blind and the leper, and I give life to the dead – by the permission of God. And I inform you of what you eat and what you store in your houses. Indeed in that is a sign for you, if you are believers.'"[13]

So these verses describe the sending of Jesus to the Children of Israel and talk about what he was going to say to them as their messenger.

---

[13] Quran 3:49.

From the previous examples we see how messengers were sent to their nations with miracles that were specific to those people and to those particular times and places. The miracle of the Quran is that it is a text, the meanings of which can be translated, and therefore can transcend a particular time or place. This served the dual purpose of being a powerful and influential miracle for a particular people while at the same time maintaining its miraculous nature for people who come afterwards.

The Arabs at the time of Muhammad were a people who were very interested in literary pursuits, specifically poetry. Their history and culture was all preserved through the medium of poetry and the honor or humiliation of a tribe was known and recorded through the quality of their poets. People were accustomed to memorizing large quantities of poems and sharing them with others. This was a gift they had and so when the Quran was revealed in a very beautiful and unique style of language which was not normal, but yet not strange, they were in awe. However, no matter how awe-inspiring this text and recitation was, they were not able to produce anything like it. Just as the miraculous change of staff to serpent of Moses was similar to a magical one and yet different, and the healing of the ill

21

of Jesus was similar to medicine but yet different, so the language of the Quran is similar to human language and yet different. The serious analyst can tell the difference and the miraculous and divine origin of the text is understood in the depths of the heart.

So Muhammad is the last of the prophets who received a miracle and a message that was timeless and could be understood and transmitted to different times and places. The finality of the prophethood of Muhammad is mentioned in the Quran where God says, "Muhammad is not the father of one of your men, but the Messenger of God and the last of the prophets. And ever is God, of all things, Knowing."[14] This leads us to the book he received, the Quran, and scripture in general.

IV. God Revealed Scriptures to Some of His Prophets

We have already stated that there were a number of messengers sent to mankind throughout history and that all of those messengers were sent with the same general

---

[14] Quran 33:40.

message of worshipping God and doing good deeds. Some of these messengers received revealed scripture and some did not. Examples of revealed scriptures would be the scrolls of Abraham, the Psalms of David, the Torah of Moses, the Gospel of Jesus, and the Quran of Muhammad. Importantly, these scriptures were not authored by the prophets themselves but were of divine origin from God. The attribution of the scriptures to various prophets is not an attribution of authorship but rather an attribution based on who received and taught it. There are many verses in the Quran that refer to earlier books, in one of them God says, "He has sent down upon you, [O Muhammad], the Book in truth, confirming what was before it. And He revealed the Torah and the Gospel before as guidance for the people. And He revealed the Quran."[15]

Muslims believe that these earlier scriptures were sources of guidance and truth in their original forms. The Quran says, "Indeed, We sent down the Torah, in which was guidance and light."[16] Also, "And We sent, following in their footsteps, Jesus, the son of Mary, confirming that which came before him in the Torah; and We gave him the

---

[15] Quran 3:3-4.
[16] Quran 5:44.

Gospel, in which was guidance and light and confirming that which preceded it of the Torah as guidance and instruction for the righteous."[17] So these scriptures are part of the legacy of revelation to human beings and the various books of scripture that we have today still contain parts of that original message.

There is, however, the important question of authenticity and preservation. It can be confidently claimed that the original messages of the Torah and the Gospel are not completely represented by the works that exist today. This incompleteness could be the result of misinterpretations, falsification, or by simply being incomplete.[18] The Quran refers to this in several places, saying:

> "And indeed, there is among them a party who alter the Scripture with their tongues so you may think it is from the Scripture, but it is not from the Scripture. And they say, 'This is from God,' but it is not from

[17] Quran 5:46.
[18] This is a long discussion and its own topic of study and is outside of the scope of this introductory work. The least that can be said is that the texts have been misinterpreted.

God. And they speak untruth about God while they know not."[19]

And God says in another place in the Quran:

"So woe to those who write the scripture with their own hands, then say, 'This is from God,' in order to exchange it for a small price. Woe to them for what their hands have written and woe to them for what they earn."[20]

These verses refer to the corruption of previous scriptures through lack of preservation as well as misinterpretation. However, Muslims do believe that in their original forms these scriptures, and particularly the Torah and the Gospel, were of a divine origin and that they contain, up to today, guidance and wisdom that is absolutely true. At the same time Muslims believe that the information that is necessary to be known from those scriptures is embodied in the Quran, which has been accurately preserved in text and meaning.

---

[19] Quran 3:78.
[20] Quran 2:79.

The book of Islam is the Quran. The Quran was revealed to the Prophet Muhammad through the intermediary of the Archangel Gabriel.[21] "The Quran" means "the recitation" and is a reference to the oral recitation and transmission of its contents. The Quran was initially learned and taught orally and the book is in its most fundamental form a recited book and not only a book to be read.

The revelation of the Quran to Muhammad began when he was forty years old. At this point in his life he had acquired the habit of retreating to the mountains outside of Mecca for contemplation and reflection. He did not know how to worship God but he knew that he disagreed with the polytheistic practices of his people. During one of these stays in the mountains the angel Gabriel came to him and told him, "Recite!" He responded by saying that he had nothing to recite. Thereafter he says that he was squeezed very hard and let go and then the exchange repeated itself three times. At the end of the third time some verses of the Quran were revealed to him and became established in his

---

[21] In Arabic *"Jibrīl."*

heart. "Recite in the name of your Lord who created. He created man from a clinging substance. Recite, and your Lord is the Most Generous, Who taught by the pen, taught man that which he knew not."[22] Muhammad's initial reaction was to rush home and seek comfort and support from his wife, Khadijah, who reassured him and sought the advice of one of her relatives who was knowledgeable about previous scriptures and the Gospel in particular.

Such was the beginning of the story of the Quran. The revelation continued from that moment until the death of the Prophet Muhammad twenty-three years later. Verses were revealed at different times and in different places and circumstances. Every time a new set of verses was revealed the Prophet was instructed as to where to put it in the order of revelation. He would then teach the scripture to his companions and followers and some of them were specifically tasked with the job of writing it down. As paper was not available in Arabia at that time, the Quran was written on many different materials such as animal bones and pieces of animal hide. As the revelation continued so did its compilation and by the time of the death of the Prophet, the Quran had reached the size of a roughly six

---

[22] Quran 96:1-5.

hundred page book. The book was memorized in its entirety by a large number of his followers and the memorization and recitation of the book is its primary mode of transmission up to today. It was shortly after his death, within two years, that the entire work was compiled into one text which was unanimously agreed upon by his followers to be authentic and reliable. It was this text that would eventually be copied and distributed to all parts of the Muslim lands.

The Quran as a text consists of 114 chapters. Roughly speaking the longer chapters are in the beginning and the chapters get shorter and shorter as the text progresses. It is not arranged according to the chronology of revelation but rather in a specific order which the Prophet Muhammad was taught by angel Gabriel. It has a very unique style in that it does not follow a strictly linear, narrative approach. It is not the story of the life of Muhammad but rather the direct speech of God to His messenger, his followers, and the rest of humanity. Sometimes it tells stories, sometimes it legislates, sometimes it comments on specific occasions. All is the address of God to His servants and every topic always ties back into the worship of God in some way. As a result its style is very unique and can only be understood by the one who experiences it.

The Quran contains scientific miracles, stories of previous nations and messengers, rules for organizing social and political life, and descriptions of God Himself. It is central to Muslim belief that the Quran is the absolute speech of God and that it has been entirely preserved in full accuracy. The Quran has the answer to all questions, but that does not mean that its followers become intellectually stagnant. A famous story to illustrate this point was with a Muslim scholar who claimed that he can answer any question using the Quran because it has the answers to everything. Someone came to him and asked him how many pieces of grain are in a huge sack of grain. His response was to call upon a baker and ask him. When he got the response he gave it to the man. He replied with astonishment because the answer was from the baker not the Quran. The scholar responded by quoting a verse from the Quran which says, "Ask those of knowledge if you know not."[23] The point of the story is to illustrate that the Quran can have answers to all things without directly addressing every question.

---

[23] Quran 16:43.

The Quran is the lasting miracle of Muhammad because of its unique preservation and its inimitable content. It differs from the miracles of previous prophets in that their miracles were limited by time and place and the Quran is not. We are not able to see the sick people that Jesus healed or the miracles of Moses which resembled magic, but we are able to read and study the Quran. This is what differentiates Islam from the other messages which came before it and makes it a message for all people in all places and times.

V. The Day of Judgment

The Day of Judgment is a time of reckoning and recompense wherein every single person will be held accountable for their deeds. Nobody knows exactly when it will come and there is nothing we can do other than prepare for it. In a famous Prophetic tradition Muhammad was once asked, "When is the Hour [the end of times or beginning of Judgment]?" He responded by saying, "What have you prepared for it?" This is the essence of the issue. Just as we came into existence and enjoy life, we too will die and after we die we will eventually be brought back to life again.

When this second coming of life occurs we will stand in front of our Lord and be asked about the things that we did while we were alive.

This is the day when all debts are settled and when the injustices of our present life are dealt with by the Most Just. It is a day that is hard to imagine in its severity and intensity. On that day God will say, "This is the day when the truthful will benefit from their truthfulness."[24] What we can say for sure about this day is that it is a day of resurrection, judgment, regret, and recompense.[25] Those who have submitted in absolute honesty and truthfulness to their Lord and done good deeds will receive the favor of their Lord, the Generous.

Anyone who understands deeply what goes on in the world on a daily basis and the types of injustices that people are subject to regularly knows that this Day must be true. If it is not true, life does not make sense. There is simply too much oppression, too much pain, and too much agony. This Day is also a hope and inspiration for those who remain steadfast and do good deeds in spite of all the

[24] Quran 5:119.
[25] These are different names that are used in the Quran to describe the Day.

31

corruption around them. It is the belief in this Day that keeps them going when times are hard and helps them to maintain their principles regardless of the consequences.

VI. Divine Decree

The last major belief is in divine decree and the infinitude of divine knowledge. The relationship between free will and determinism is an age old one that has many consequences for how people perceive the world that they live in. The stance of Islam is a middle ground in between the two.

Islam basically teaches that there are some things that are decreed by God, but at the same time human beings have the ability and responsibility to exercise free will and choice in relation to the situations that they face. This essentially means that there are many things that we have control over and some things that we do not. We do not know the time when we will die, we do not know how much wealth we will have and what kind of worldly circumstances we will be born into, but we also have the ability and responsibility to act within the circumstances that we have been presented with to try and make the best of our situation. It is God who judges us based on our choices and actions with infinite wisdom and knowledge. He does not judge us based on our results, but rather based on our efforts.

In the practical daily life of a Muslim this translates to an understanding about material circumstances that eases the individual's perspective on hardships and motivates them to act in the most principled way possible regardless of their situation. If someone believes that God has written for them a certain amount of income and if He wills for them not to receive it, they will not receive it and that will help them to still deal ethically in their financial transactions. They know unethical transactions will not increase their wealth, rather if anything it will decrease the blessings in their wealth. If they believe that the length of their life is determined they will be more likely to have patience in the face of the tragedy of losing a loved one than if they did not. In this way, these beliefs in divine decree give the person a level of strength and determination to deal with the uncertainties of life while at the same time pushing them to live with righteousness.

Summary

These are the basic six beliefs of Islam. They are the core of the Muslim theology. Muslims believe that these same principles were taught by every prophet that was sent to mankind regardless of time or place. Anyone who believes in these principles, as simple as they seem, is a Muslim; and anyone who disbelieves in any of these principles is not a Muslim. It is the foundation that everything else is built upon. They are, again, in summary: God is One, angels exist, God sent messengers to mankind, some of those messengers brought scripture, the Day of Judgment is true, and divine decree.

Pillars of Practice

One of the core beliefs in Islam is that it is not enough to simply profess faith in something but that action must necessarily follow from such a proclamation. As such it is important that we discuss the core actions of Islam after covering the major beliefs. Those core actions are five: the declaration of faith, ritual prayer, almsgiving, fasting in Ramadan, and making pilgrimage to Mecca once in a lifetime if possible.

I. The Declaration of Faith

The first pillar of practice in the teachings of Islam is the declaration of faith. This is for the person to state, "I bear witness that there is no god but One God, and I bear witness that Muhammad was His servant and messenger." It is by this statement that the unbeliever enters into the faith of Islam and it is this statement that the Muslim repeats on a regular basis as a reminder to himself.

The subtle thing about this statement is that although it is very brief it is also very powerful and complex. Through the statement the individual is denying the existence of any and all partners that are associated with God and then affirming His existence. It is to clear out all impurities of belief and then to establish the ultimate truth. In the second part of the declaration the person is witnessing to the prophethood of Muhammad. In doing so they are acknowledging not only Muhammad but the entire lineage of prophets throughout history. They are also declaring who their role model is in the decisions they make in life. Everything stems from the declaration of faith and from there it is a continual process of trying to come closer to God through following the example of His messenger. For this reason the entirety of Islam can be said to be summed up in this simple yet profound statement.

II. Ritual Prayer (*Şalāh*)

The second major action of faith and the most important action of faith is the ritual prayer. It is common to find people confused as to what Muslims mean when they talk about prayer. This is because there are many types of prayers in the teachings of Islam but the one that is referred to here is a very particular type of worship and that is why I referred to it as the ritual prayer. We also consider the mere act of speaking directly to God to be a type of prayer, as is the act of raising one's hands and asking God for whatever it is they desire. There are also types of prayers to be said at different times and places throughout the day such as when one rides their car or when they leave their home. All of these are simple and fluid types of prayer but the ritual prayer is different. Its actions and statements are strictly defined and it has a certain way that it must be done at specified times of the day.

The ritual prayer is the most important pillar of Islam and it occurs five times daily. The whole process of the prayer takes anywhere from five to ten minutes under normal circumstances and must be performed during particular slots of time during the day. The first prayer is performed between dawn and sunrise. The second is performed between midday and mid-afternoon. The third is performed between mid-afternoon and sunset. The fourth is performed between sunset and when it gets dark. And the fifth is performed between the time when it becomes dark and the following dawn. The person has the choice as to where and when they pray those ritual prayers within the time slots and they can perform the prayer individually or in congregation. Prayers do not have to be performed in the mosque but it is good for congregants to attend the mosque as regularly as they can.

The ritual prayer is composed of units that repeat themselves for a number of times that varies depending on which prayer it is that the person is praying. The prayer starts with the person standing facing Mecca and saying "God is greater" while raising their hands. This action signifies their entering into the prayer and their leaving behind any of their worldly distractions or concerns. Thereafter they praise God and then read a selection from the Quran by memory. This selection does not have any set limit other than that it should be at least a few short verses in length and it should begin with the opening chapter of the Quran. After this they say "God is greater" again and move into a bowing position. In this position they say "Glorified is my Lord the Most Great" three times and then rise back to a standing position saying, "God hears the one who praises Him." Here they say, "Our Lord to you belongs all praise" and then say "God is greater" and move to a position of prostration. While prostrating they say, "Glorified is my Lord the Most High." Then they say, "God is greater" and move to a sitting position. From there they say "God is greater" and move to prostration again, repeating the previous statement. After the second prostration they say, "God is greater" and rise to return to the initial standing position. This whole process signifies the completion of one unit of prayer and the ritual prayers vary between two to four units. As one can easily see the prayer is entirely centered on the worship of God and submission to Him and His will. It is an act of pure devotion.

There are many types of worship in Islam that could be referred to as prayer. These include calling upon God, discoursing with Him directly, and various invocations that are meant to be said at certain times and in certain places. These are all integral parts of the spiritual life of the Muslim but they are not what most Muslims are referring to when they talk about prayer, and definitely not what they are talking about in the context of the pillars of Islam. In such discussions prayer is referring to the ritual worship that was described above.

III. Almsgiving (*Zakāh*)

As a general rule there is a heavy emphasis on charity in the teachings of Islam. Texts indicate that even the simplest of things can be considered charity, such as clearing an object from the street or smiling in the face of another person. This charity also takes the form of spending money and resources. The *zakah* is a very particular type of charity that is levied on a person's wealth. The meaning of the word in Arabic connotes 'growth' and 'purification.' The idea is that when someone gives from the charity that is due upon them for the uplifting of their brothers and sisters it is an act of growth and purification for them and their wealth. It applies to resources such as money, trade goods, livestock, and agriculture. The *zakah* is a mandatory charity upon a person who has a certain amount of wealth for at least one year. In the case of monetary wealth the amount of charity is 2.5% of one's savings and in the case of agriculture it can vary between 5% and 10% which is paid each time the crops are harvested.

God specifically lays out who the eligible recipients of *zakah* are in the ninth chapter of the Quran:

> "*Zakah* expenditures are only for the poor
> and the needy and for those employed to
> collect [*zakah*] and for bringing hearts
> together [for Islam] and for freeing slaves
> and for those in debt and for the cause of
> God and for the traveler – an obligation
> [imposed] by God. And God is Knowing
> and Wise."[26]

The verse mentions eight categories of people who are allowed to receive this specific charity. The first is those who are in a serious state of poverty and need. They are the people who are struggling to pay the rent and cannot find enough food to eat. The second is for those who are employed in the collection of the charity itself. The third is for the bringing of hearts together. This can be interpreted to be a donation that is given to non-Muslims who seem to be interested in Islam or also to new Muslims as an encouragement and support to them. The forth is in the emancipation of slaves. Slavery was a major and widespread social and economic institution at the time of the Prophet Muhammad. Although the teachings of Islam did not outright forbid slavery they did systematically push

---

[26] Quran 9:60.

towards the abolishment of slavery. The fifth is for those who are in debt. In Islam debt is something that is allowed as long as it is not accompanied by interest, but people are encouraged not to stay in debt. One of the ways to overcome the smothering nature of debt is to use this charity to help pay off debts. The sixth is in the cause of God, which classically meant to support a just war. Some scholars, especially modern ones, have taken this to also apply to institutions and organizations that are on the forefront of preserving and promoting Islam in places where its adherents are few in numbers. The seventh is for the traveler. This means the charity can be spent to support a traveler who has become stranded on his journey and needs some extra support to make it back home.

These are the categories that *zakah* can be distributed to and there can be no adding to these categories. One is required to spend this particular type of charity on these groups of people and they cannot spend it on their own dependents. The spirit of the charity is to promote the circulation of wealth in society and for the wealthy to support those who are struggling by means of their charitable contributions.

IV. Fasting (*Ṣiyām*)

Fasting is a spiritual development practice that is found across many cultures and religions. Different peoples and faiths partake in it in different ways. The fast of Islam is to refrain from food, drink, and marital relations from the time of dawn until sunset. It can be done throughout the year with the exception of a few days when one is not supposed to fast. However, the fast that is considered one of the pillars of the practice of Islam is the fast of the month of Ramadan.

Ramadan is the most sacred month of the year in the Muslim calendar. The Muslim calendar is a lunar calendar so it is slightly different than the typical Gregorian calendar that is in use around much of the world today. The year in the lunar calendar is about ten days shorter than the year in the solar calendar and so the month of Ramadan shifts slightly each year in relation to the seasons. This means that roughly every 35 years Ramadan will shift through all of the seasons. At the time of writing this in 2014, Ramadan falls in the summer and so the fasts are longer but after a few years it will move into the spring and then winter and the days will be shorter.

Many look at the fast of Ramadan, which does not even permit water, and think that it is very difficult. However, the body adjusts quickly and Muslims get great enjoyment and spiritual enlightenment out of the month. It is a time of family, worship, and celebrating God. There have even been professional athletes who have observed the fast while competing. Perhaps the most famous example of this is Hakeem Olajuwon who fasted while playing in the NBA. He was still able to compete and even excel and was named Player of the Month in February 1995, even though Ramadan had begun in that month.

The core spiritual ideal behind fasting is that during it the person detaches from that which would normally be allowed, namely food, drink, and marital relations for the sake of attaching to a higher ideal, seeking the pleasure of their Lord. In doing so one recognizes and develops their capacity to resist, the ability to control oneself, which is so central to the process of spiritual development and worship. It is this reason that makes the month so important and makes it a reminder and opportunity for all believers to turn back to God.

V. The Pilgrimage (*Ḥajj*)

The pilgrimage, or *hajj* in Arabic, is a yearly ritual
that occurs during the period of a couple of weeks in the
Muslim calendar month of Dhul Hijjah. The rites of the
pilgrimage were initially performed by the Prophet
Abraham and it was the teaching of Muhammad to revive
these rites. The spirit and rites of the pilgrimage revolve
around the story of Abraham and his son Ishmael. Abraham
was married to Sarah and although they were older in age
they had not yet conceived a child. In light of the situation,
Abraham married Hagar and they had a son together.
Muslims have debated whether that first born was Ishmael
or Isaac but the stronger stance is that it was Ishmael.
Shortly thereafter Abraham was ordered by God to take his
wife, Hagar, and son, Ishmael, to a deserted portion of
Arabia. This land later became the city of Mecca. In the
story mother and child are left in this desolate place and
although Hagar is worried she is also content with the will
of God. Knowing that they are in need of water she decides
to run up to the highest nearby hill and look for any sign of
life. She finds none. Then she descends and climbs another
nearby hill and again finds nothing. She then went back and
forth between these hills a total of seven times. This

journey between the two hills is what is called in Arabic *al-sa'iy* and it is one of the key elements of the pilgrimage rites. Another major rite of pilgrimage is to circle around the black house, *al-ka'bah,* which is in the middle of the sacred mosque. This structure was built by Abraham and Ishmael, by direct command from God, as the first house of worship for human beings.

The last major rite of the pilgrimage is related to the great event of the relationship between Abraham and his son that inspires the whole act of worship: his willingness to sacrifice his son. This act of Abraham's was an act of total and complete submission and is symbolic of the relationship between the worshipper and their Lord. The Muslim version of the story is slightly different in that Abraham did not go on this path alone with his son not knowing what was going on. In the Muslim tradition he actually tells his son that he has seen in a dream that he is to sacrifice him. The son, knowing that the dreams of prophets are true, tells his father that he should do what he was commanded to do without concern because he will find him patient in the face of this great test. So they go together to the place of sacrifice and when the time comes Abraham is told that he has done what he was commanded and that he does not have to sacrifice his son, but rather an animal instead. This act of pure submission is the core message of Islam and the reason why the pilgrimage is such an important pillar of Muslim life.

The pilgrimage is an obligation that is to be performed once in a lifetime for those who are capable of doing so. If one does not have the money or the health to go, or the route of journey is unsafe, they are freed from this obligation. However, throughout history people have traveled from all different parts of the world to make pilgrimage to this holy site and it is one of the great symbols of Islam. Today there are roughly three or four million people who make this pilgrimage each year. They all come in unity and submission to their Creator, seeking His pleasure. It is a great sight of human unity and equality as all of the male pilgrims are required to dress in the same way, wearing no more than two pieces of seamless cloth and some slippers. It is truly an amazing and inspirational scene. One of the most famous American figures to be impacted by the pilgrimage was Malcolm X. He said about it:

> There were tens of thousands of pilgrims, from all over the world. They were of all

colors, from blue-eyed blondes to black-skinned Africans. But we were all participating in the same ritual, displaying a spirit of unity and brotherhood that my experiences in America had led me to believe never could exist between the white and the non-white. America needs to understand Islam, because this is the one religion that erases from its society the race problem. You may be shocked by these words coming from me. But on this pilgrimage, what I have seen, and experienced, has forced me to rearrange much of my thought patterns previously held.[27]

Summary

These are the pillars of practice in Islam. Every Muslim who professes to believe in God and His messenger is expected to fulfill these pillars and try to their utmost ability to be consistent in performing them. They are simple

[27] Excerpted from *The Autobiography of Malcolm X.*

acts but of the utmost importance. Some are highly individual acts of worship but at the same time none are free from the spirit of community. All acts are meant to attach people directly to their Creator but also to be performed in the context of the development of a community of believers. Prayer is one's personal connection with their Lord but at the same time it is recommended to perform it in congregation. Almsgiving is about purifying and increasing one's wealth but at the same time it gives support to the community. Fasting is very personal and only God knows the truth about the quality of one's fast, but it occurs in the context of a month of community and celebration of God through congregational worship. The pilgrimage is an act of submission like none other, but it is done in unity with a large group of believers. All are personal and yet communal, such is the balance and spirit of Islam.

Conclusion

There is much confusion about the teachings of Islam around the world these days. It is not only non-Muslims who have misconceptions, but Muslims as well. What I have sought to do in this small work is to outline the major beliefs and practices of Islam. These few pages are the foundation. They are the main things that the Muslim should believe and the major things that they should be focusing their practice of Islam around. There are additional acts of worship and beliefs that should be followed but they are all secondary to the foundational ones. My hope is for this booklet to be a simple introduction to Islam for those who are interested in knowing more about it and as an easy refresher or base for those Muslims who are trying to reestablish their faith. Any good is solely from God and any mistakes are mine.